100 QUESTIONS about DINOSAURS

and all the answers too!

Written and Illustrated by
Simon Abbott

PETER PAUPER PRESS, INC.
White Plains, New York

PETER PAUPER PRESS

In 1928, at the age of twenty-two, Peter Beilenson began printing books on a small press in the basement of his parents' home in Larchmont, New York. Peter—and later, his wife, Edna—sought to create fine books that sold at "prices even a pauper could afford."

Today, still family owned and operated, Peter Pauper Press continues to honor our founders' legacy of quality, value, and fun for big kids and small kids alike.

to joshua
Who knows all there is to know about dinosaurs!

Designed by Heather Zschock

Text and illustrations copyright © 2018 by Simon Abbott

Published by Peter Pauper Press, Inc.
202 Mamaroneck Avenue
White Plains, New York 10601 USA

Published in the United Kingdom and Europe by Peter Pauper Press, Inc.
c/o White Pebble International
Unit 2, Plot 11 Terminus Rd.
Chichester, West Sussex PO19 8TX, UK

Library of Congress Cataloging-in-Publication Data Available

ISBN 978-1-4413-2848-9
Manufactured for Peter Pauper Press, Inc.
Printed in China

7 6 5 4 3

Visit us at www.peterpauper.com

WELCOME TO THE GREAT DINOSAUR DISCOVERY!

These awesome creatures ruled the Earth
for over 165 million years!

Let's get the inside story and dig up some
dirt on these deadly dinosaurs!

Were all dinos pea-brained, meat-munching monsters?

How big did these colossal creatures get?

Why aren't the dinosaurs still stomping
and sprinting across Earth today?

It's time for our amazing adventure to begin!

Turn the page, and step back millions of years to
uncover the dinosaur data!

DINO DATES

Let's follow the dinos' journey from resourceful reptiles, to Earth's dominant creatures, to eventual extinction. What an adventure!

When did dinosaurs begin to trample and tread around the planet?
Over 230 million years ago! They evolved from other reptiles during a time on Earth called the *Mesozoic* era.

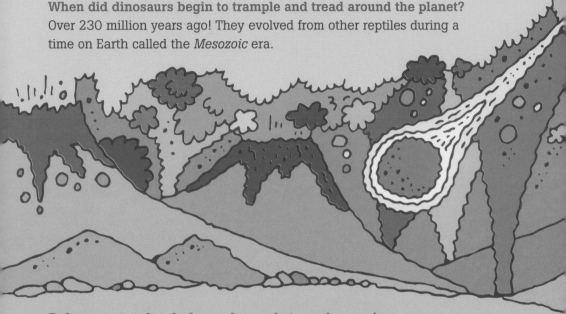

Before we get ahead of ourselves, what was happening before the dinos checked in?
Not great news, I'm afraid. Let's hear it for the *Permian mass extinction*!

I've got bad vibes about that! Was it as dreadful as it sounds?
Put it this way: The nickname for the *Permian mass extinction* is **The Great Dying**. A massive 95 percent of sea- and 70 percent of land-based species were wiped out. Funnily, many fungi came out of this fiasco just fine.

Why did the fungi leave the party?

Sounds epic! What caused this catastrophe?
It happened 248 million years ago, so my memory is a little hazy! Seriously, though, there are a few theories bouncing about. Take your pick from an asteroid impact, a massive methane gas release from microbes, a drop in oxygen levels, huge changes in Earth's temperatures, vast volcanic eruptions, or a deadly mix of these devastating events.

How do we go from global disaster to the great dino dynasty?
A group of animals called *Archosaurs* was one of the lucky ones that survived. They were a tough bunch of reptiles that swooped into the abandoned feeding grounds. These go-getters were the dinosaurs' ancient ancestors!

there wasn't mushroom!

HOW LONG WAS THE MESOZOIC?

Take a look at the timeline! It lasted over 180 million years. This era is split into three chunks of time: the Triassic, the Jurassic, and the Cretaceous periods.

Why is the Mesozoic period divided into three sections?
Each period experienced major shifts. The planet's land transformed, new creatures and plants developed, and Earth saw big climate changes.

TRIASSIC Dinosaurs evolve JURASSIC

248
MILLION YEARS AGO

206
MILLION YEARS AGO

 WHEN?

TRIASSIC
(252 – 201 million years ago)

 EARTH

One land mass

 WEATHER

Hot and dry

 CREATURES

The first dinosaurs and small mammals appeared.

 PLANTS

Ferns, conifers, and horsetails

 BIG NEWS

The Triassic began and ended in a world-wide extinction.

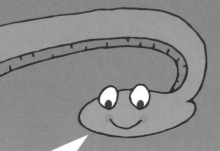

What do you call someone who just *won't* stop talking about prehistoric creatures?

A dino-bore!

How long were dinosaurs on Earth?
They first appeared during the late *Triassic* period, so let's estimate that they plodded around the planet for between 165 to 177 million years. (Spoiler alert! They were living on Earth longer than they've been extinct!) By comparison, the human species, *Homo sapiens,* have only been around for a mere 200,000 years!

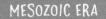

Birds evolve

CRETACEOUS

Flowering plants appear

End of the prehistoric dinos!

Humans evolve

144
MILLION YEARS AGO

65
MILLION YEARS AGO

NOW!

WHEN?	**JURASSIC** (201 – 145 million years ago)	WHEN?	**CRETACEOUS** (145 – 66 million years ago)
EARTH	Land mass began to break apart.	EARTH	Continued to break apart, causing volcanic activity
WEATHER	Hot and dry, then humid with large, flooded areas	WEATHER	Warm, with high sea levels
CREATURES	Dinosaur species got larger, and flying lizards called pterosaurs took to the sky.	CREATURES	The first ants, grasshoppers, and butterflies evolve.
PLANTS	Forests grew quickly in the warm and moist conditions.	PLANTS	The first flowering plants appeared.
BIG NEWS	The first primitive bird appeared.	BIG NEWS	The end of the Cretaceous period means the end of the dinosaurs.

Did dinosaurs share the planet with early cavemen?
All together now! 1...2...3...NO!

After the dinosaurs fizzled out (more on that later!), it was nearly 65 million years before early man dropped by.

HOME, SWEET HOME!

What kind of world did dinosaurs inhabit? Did they laze on the beach, tramp through forests, or chill on a mountaintop? Let's find out what the dinos called home!

What did planet Earth look like when the dinosaurs first evolved?
In the Triassic, there were no continents or countries—just one massive chunk of land called Pangaea. This was surrounded by a single ocean called *Panthalassa*.

One slab of land called Pangaea

North America

Eurasia (Will split to become Europe and Asia)

Africa

India

South America

Australia

Antarctica

One ocean called Panthalassa

LOOK FAMILIAR?
This is how Earth appears today!

Wow! A supercontinent! What was it like there?
The interior of Pangaea would have been covered by a hot, dry desert, as it was so far from the sea and surrounded by mountain ranges that shut out rainfall. A dense tropical rainforest, similar to the Amazon jungle, grew near Earth's equator, and the planet's warmer temperatures would mean no freezing ice caps.

No ice caps! Does this mean that dinos could stomp around Antarctica too?
Yes, and we have the proof! Eager scientists used a plane, ship, helicopter, and inflatable boat to reach dino fossils, such as *Antarctopelta*, on exhausting Antarctic expeditions.

8

What other dino hotspots are worth checking out?

The slow break up of Earth's land mass during the time of the dinosaurs means that evidence of these prehistoric creatures is found all over the world. Dino finds have been unearthed by fossil hunters in every single continent, including the *Tyrannosaurus rex* in North America, *Spinosaurus* in Egypt, and *Velociraptor* in Russia.

How did Earth as we know it begin to take shape from a single slab of land?

Over the 165 million years that dinosaurs were alive, the supercontinent, Pangaea, began to break apart.

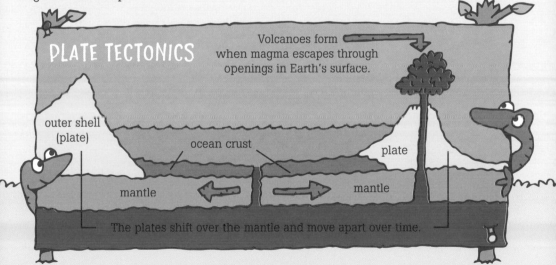

PLATE TECTONICS

Volcanoes form when magma escapes through openings in Earth's surface.

outer shell (plate)

ocean crust

plate

mantle

mantle

The plates shift over the mantle and move apart over time.

Break apart! Was this another asteroid impact?

No! It's down to *plate tectonics*. Earth's outer shell is fractured into several large pieces or plates, which shift over Earth's layer of moving rock, called the *mantle*.

How long did it take for Earth to look how it does now?

It's taken 200 million years to get to where we are today!

How did all of this moving around affect the dinosaurs?
Volcanoes formed as the plates moved apart, releasing masses of carbon dioxide into the atmosphere, making temperatures hot and humid. Forests covered much of the planet. This was a great food source for the greedy dinosaurs!

Were dinosaurs Earth's only inhabitants during the Mesozoic?
Let's take a roll call! Lizards and crocodiles were first in line. Insects, similar to today's beetles, were eventually joined by flies, bees, and wasps. Small mammals shared the earth, and marine life, including turtles, sharks, and hagfish, swam in the warm sea.

10

What plants could the dinosaurs spot as they looked around their patch?
Large dinos could munch on a bountiful supply of slow-growing conifer trees.
In the southern areas on Earth, *cycadophtes* **(SIGH-cah-dough-fights)** would grow.
These are seed plants, with woody trunks and large, stiff leaves. Another dino food
source would be the ginkgo tree. These plants have existed for around 270 million
years, and would pop up on higher ground. Dinosaurs living in damp and humid
conditions would have been able to feast on ferns. Delicious!

DINO DICTIONARY!

It's time to nail down these strange-looking specimens with even stranger names! Let's get the dinosaurs to fall into line, so we can inspect them close-up!

What does the word "dinosaur" actually mean?
It's a mix of the two Greek words, *deinos* meaning "terrible," and *saurus* which means "lizard." Terrible lizard!

~~CREEPY CREATURE~~ X   ~~REVOLTING REPTILE~~ X   *How rude!* TERRIBLE LIZARD ✓

How did each dino that was discovered get its name?
Dinosaur names were often put together from Greek, Latin, or more recently Chinese words. Here's one you may have heard of:

TRI
It's Latin for three

CERAT
That's Greek for horn

OPS
Another Greek word meaning face

What do you get when you put them together?
TRI-CERAT-OPS!

Were dinosaurs named in any other way?
Some specimens were named after the location where the fossilized creatures were unearthed. Can you guess where the *Utahraptor* was found? Other dinosaur hunters named their finds after people, such as *Diplodocus carnegii*, which was named after Andrew Carnegie, the man who funded the diplodocus discoverers' expedition!

Can you name 10 dinosaurs in 10 seconds?

Yes! 8 triceratops and 2 stegosaurus!

How can we arrange the dinosaur species into groups?
Scientists divide dinosaurs into several big groups.
Here are two of them:

THEROPODS (meaning beast feet)

How did it move?
On two back legs.
(Their front legs had sharp claws
for grasping victims.)

What were its stand-out features?
A large head, strong jaw, and sharp teeth

SAUROPODS (meaning lizard feet)

How did it move?
On 4 sturdy legs, of equal size

What were its stand-out features?
A small head, and long neck,
with flat, peg-like teeth

THEROPODS
TYRANNOSAURUS
TROODON
ALLOSAURUS
VELOCIRAPTOR
SPINOSAURUS

MY TOP 5!

SAUROPODS
DIPLODOCUS
BRACHIOSAURUS
AMPHICOELIAS
ARGENTINOSAURUS
SALTASAURUS

MY TOP 5!

PREHISTORIC PLAYOFFS!

Who wins the First Dino on Earth award?

Well, for years, the *Eoraptor (EE-oh-RAP-tor)* has taken first place as the earliest known dinosaur. This little specimen was found in 231 million year old Argentinian rock. However, scientists have identified a potential dino that roamed Africa about 10 million years *before* the *Eoraptor*. Let's hear it for (take a deep breath) *Nyasasaurus parringtoni* (NYE-as-ah-SORE-uhs PARE-ring-toe-nee). It's thought that this creature stood upright, measuring half the height of an adult giraffe.

Which dinos grab the awards for the biggest and the smallest?

Currently, the record-holder for biggest dino is the awesome Patagotitan (PAT-ah-goh-TIE-ton). At 120 feet (37 m) long, this bulky beast was longer than four fire trucks put together.

One of the Mesozoic's tiniest dinosaurs was the chicken-sized *Compsognathus* (comp-SOG-nah-thus), which stood about 3 feet tall (1 m). Congratulations!

Now for a blood-thirsty battle. Who's the first-placed fighting machine?

Runner-up prize goes to the "scythe lizard" *Therizinosaurus* (there-ih-ZEEN-oh-SORE-us), who wielded three enormous curved claws (although as ferocious as they looked, these claws were probably used for digging).

The fighting champion has to be the *Tyrannosaurus rex* (tie-RAN-oh-SORE-us REX). This ruthless creature had over 50 banana-sized teeth. The power of its bite is estimated at three times the force of a great white shark.

Onto the armored division! Who's the top dino-defender?

Silver medal goes to the *Triceratops* (tri-SAIR-ah-tops), a defensive dinosaur near the top of its game. The hard, bony neck frill shielded its soft, exposed body.

At the top of the podium is the *Ankylosaurus* (an-KIE-loh-sore-us). This striking specimen displayed a rugged body shield, with hard plates and bony spikes running from head to toe. Attackers had to watch out for the serious-looking club at the end of its whirling tail too!

Who gets the Weirdest-Looking Dino award?

With its dome-like skull, the knuckleheaded *Colepiocephale* (COH-leh-pee-oh-SEH-fehl) snags second place. Top marks go to the Parasaurolophus (para-SORE-awe-LOW-fuss). It's famous for the hollow, tube-like crest on top of its head, through which it could likely holler and howl.

Ready for the speed sprint? Who wins the dino dash?

3...2...1...go! Running into the distance goes the *Ornithomimid* (OR-nih-thoh-MY-mid), who could probably clock up speeds of up to 50 miles per hour (80 km per hour) to escape from a ravenous rival. That's faster than a greyhound! Time to race over to the next page...

A DINO'S DAY!

What did a dino do from dawn till dusk? Time to get the low-down on their daily routine!

How did a dinosaur fill its day?
Eating! A 4-ton African elephant spends up to 18 hours a day chowing down, so just imagine how long it takes to fill up an 80-ton *Argentinosaurus*!

FACT OR FICTION

Is it true that all dinosaurs were meat-munching monsters?
That's way off the mark! In fact, only a small percentage of dinos are thought to have been meat-eaters, or *carnivores* **(CAR-nih-vors)**. The rest filled up on plants. These dinosaurs are called *herbivores* **(ERB-ih-vors)**.

Did any greedy dinos eat meat AND plants?
Sure! These creatures are called *omnivores* **(AHM-ni-vors)**, and probably include the dinosaurs *Ornithomimus* and *Oviraptor*. They may have chowed down on plants, eggs, and insects.

How could I spot the difference between a meat-eater and a plant lover? Let's take a look at some common traits!

CARNIVORES

- Super-strong legs to run and catch their suppers
- Sharp teeth and a forceful jaw
- Great eyesight and sense of smell
- A big brain to plan the capture

HERBIVORES

- Wide, blunt, flat teeth like pegs
- Ate by grinding and stripping vegetation
- Very long necks to allow them to grab leaves from tall trees

Here comes a hungry Tyrannosaurus rex.
What would its daily diet consist of?
Anything! It would hunt and devour dinos, even crunching
their bones, or scavenge the carcasses of dead dinos. It likely
needed to consume more than 40,000 calories a day, so if it
was alive today, it could make do with about 80 hamburgers.

How much food did the huge herbivores need each day?
Scientists have done the sums and estimate that these
dinosaurs would need 100,000 calories a day, or
around 1,000 pounds (455 kg) of ferns, conifers,
leaves, and moss.

Burp!

**That's a lot of plants! How could a dinosaur eat 1,000
pounds of vegetation in one day?**
Many of them simply spent a lot of time eating! However,
some herbivores often gobbled plants whole, without
chewing, along with stones called *gastroliths*. These
gastroliths would have helped to break down vegetation
inside the dinosaur's stomach.

Important question. Did dinosaurs fart?
Probably! Experts have done the math and estimate that the dinosaur
population could have produced over 570 million tons of gas each year.

Another serious question. How big was a dinosaur's poop?
If we're going to be serious, then the proper word for a fossilized poop is a
coprolite (that's Greek for "dung stone"). Scientists have been looking at these
fossilized feces for years to work out what ancient animals ate. They calculate that
a *Tyrannosaurus rex* would have pooped around 2.5 liters a day, and the vast
Argentinosaurus would have off-loaded a whopping 15 liters. That's bigger than
a basketball!

Why did carnivorous
dinosaurs eat
raw meat?

Because they
didn't have a
barbecue!

Let's talk prehistoric parenting! How were baby dinosaurs born?
Female dinosaurs laid up to 21 eggs in a hole, or a mud-rimmed nest mound.

What was dino childcare like?
Some dinosaurs may have buried their eggs, then scurried off. Others, such as the
Maiasaura (meaning "good mother lizard"), built nest colonies and may have fed
their mini dinos chewed up plants after they hatched.

What did these dinosaur eggs look like?
All shapes and sizes! Some were small, like tennis balls, and others were as big
as soccer balls. Some eggs were round, and some were elongated with the length
three times longer than the width.

How did giant sauropods lay eggs without breaking them?
Good question! Even if these colossal creatures crouched down, they'd still
be eight feet (two meters) off the ground! Scientists think that the eggs
would have been laid through a tube, extending to the ground
from the female dino's body. Some modern-day turtles
use a similar method.

What makes more
noise than a baby
dinosaur?

two baby
dinosaurs!

#1
MOM

How old did dinos get?

It seems that the bigger and slower a creature is, the longer it lives. Take "Sue," the eight-ton *T-rex* whose skeleton is on display at the Field Museum, Chicago. Looking at the growth rings on her bones, it is calculated that she lived for 28 years. However, it's thought that the 40-ton, 85-foot (26-meter) long *Brachiosaurus* may have reached its hundredth birthday. Congratulations, old-timer!

I'm almost an old fossil!

100 TODAY!

The sun is setting on the dinosaur's day.
How did a dog-tired dino get some rest?

Like a handful of dinosaur data, we're not too sure! What we know for sure is that some dinos curled up to sleep. The *Mei long* (meaning sleeping dragon) dinosaur skeleton was found in China, with its head settled on its tucked-in arms, and the tail curled around its body. Sweet dreams!

PREHISTORIC SKIES AND SEAS!

Dinosaurs weren't alone on this hot and humid planet. Let's take off, dive in, and check out some spine-chilling sea creatures and fearsome flying reptiles!

What was prehistoric life beneath the waves like?
The ocean was swarming! There were speedy plesiosaurs, giant crocodiles, sharks, squid-like cephalopods **(SEH-fah-low-pods)**, and coral reefs.

Who wins the "Oddest in the Ocean" award?
That would be the *Temnodontosaurus* **(TEM-noh-DAWN-toe-SORE-us)**. This dolphin-looking creature weighed in at 5 tons and measured about 30 feet (9 m) long. That's longer than a great white shark! The *Temnodontosaurus* is famous for its huge eyes, measuring 10 inches (25 cm) wide!

Who made light work of lunch?
In second place is the *Thalassomedon* **(tha-LASS-oh-don)**, a 40 foot (12 m) monster whose flipper was longer than an average human! Its 20-foot-long (6-meter-long) neck likely helped it to surprise and swallow huge shoals of fish from its hiding place in the ocean depths.

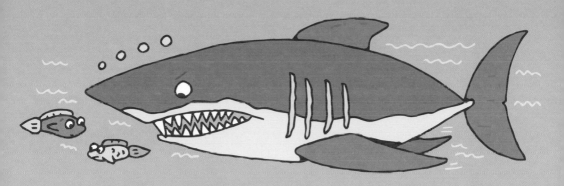

Who gets the honors in the "Fastest Freestyle"?
The *Liopleurodon* (LIE-oh-PLOOR-oo-dawn) swam at a speedy 25 miles per hour (40 km per hour). This mean-looking marine reptile was half the length of a bowling alley and had a 5-foot-long (1.5-m-long) skull filled with razor-sharp teeth.

Did the Liopleurodon have any other specialities that might make waves?
Yes! A great sense of smell! It's thought that this sea creature funnelled water through its nostrils and picked up chemicals produced by its nervous victims.

What should you do if you spot a liopleurodon?

Start swimming!

It seems that all sea creatures we've talked about so far aimed to terrify.
Did any prehistoric marine life adopt a more relaxed approach?
Sure! The chilled-out giant turtle *Archelon* probably took long naps on the ocean floor and occasionally drifted onto the surface to feed.

LOOK UP, DINOS!

Time to swoop in and get the low-down on the gliding creatures taking flight.

What were the first non-bug animals to take flight?
These flying reptiles are called *pterosaurs* **(TEH-row-sores)**, and lived at the same time as the dinosaurs.

How did these non-dino creatures take off?
They probably took a standing jump, using all four limbs and the leathery sheet of skin and muscle that stretched from their longer fourth fingers to their ankles.

> Which prehistoric animal was the scariest?

> the terror-dactyl!

Did pterosaurs have feathers to help them fly?
No, but they were probably covered in fine, fur-like fibers.

Cool! What other features helped them fly?
As the pterosaurs evolved, their bones became hollow and filled with air. This kept them lightweight, making it easier to get airborne!

What did pterosaurs eat?
Some pterosaurs would swoop low over water, gobbling up fish. *Pterodaustro* **(tair-oh-DOW-strow)** had teeth that acted as a "comb," filtering out mini morsels.

Welcome to the Flying Hall of Fame! First, who's in the running for the "One-of-a-kind" award?

A strong contender is the *Pteranodon* (tair-AHN-oh-dawn). This strange specimen was as tall as an adult, and had a toothless beak and a bony crest. Some experts think this curious crest was used to show off!

Who else could be nominated?

Well, my vote goes to the remarkable *Tapejara* (TAP-ah-JAR-ah). Just look at the colorful crest on the top of its head, which would be used to attract mates! Its downward curving beak may have been used for nibbling on fruit, or for scooping up fish.

Which flying reptile grabs gold in the "Sky-high" section?

The *Quetzalcoatlus* (ket-zel-KWAH-toe-lus) was as tall as a giraffe and had a massive wing span of 36 feet. This formidable flying machine would have been able to carry off an average sized, but very frightened, human.

At the other end of the scale, who flies off with the "Teeny-tiny Trophy"?

Anurognathus (an-NEW-rog-NAY-thus) was only the size of a woodpecker! This pocket-sized pterosaur was probably the perfect size for hunting insects.

THE DAWN OF THE DINOSAURS!

Let's take a trip back to the Triassic era and welcome the very first dinosaurs.

What kind of world would these prehistoric prototypes inhabit?
The Triassic period began after the worst mass extinction ever, but though it took some time for the planet to recover, this new world provided an opportunity for a new group of animals to evolve: the dinosaurs!

What were Triassic conditions like?
This era is defined by dry heat and warm seas. Dinosaurs kept away from the dusty deserts, living in the more fertile coastal areas.

What did dinos eat on this parched planet?
The early dinosaurs were adaptable. They feasted on early mammals, and even each other! Over time, the warm seas became crammed with life, and dinosaurs had their pick of tasty sharks, marine reptiles, and fish.

What about the herbivores? What were the vegetarian options?
Triassic plants formed tough, waxy coverings to stop them from drying out in the relentless heat. The versatile dinos developed large, flat, blunt teeth that were designed to rip, tear, shred, and chew this unappetizing greenery.

How did the Triassic end?
The Triassic-Jurassic mass extinction! Not too much to worry about, though. It only ranks number four in the five major extinction events that the planet has endured. Phew!

So, did the dinosaurs survive?
I'll say! Although many of the land and sea species were wiped out, it opened the door for the dinosaurs to diversify and grow in size.

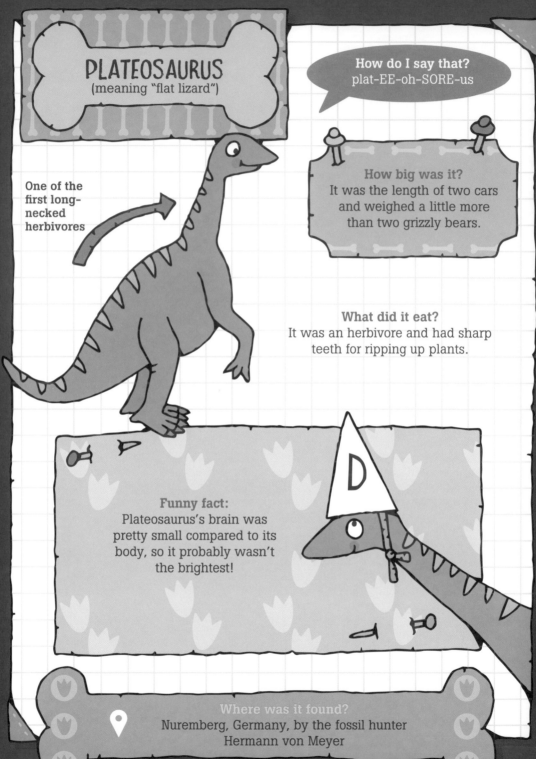

PLATEOSAURUS
(meaning "flat lizard")

How do I say that?
plat-EE-oh-SORE-us

One of the first long-necked herbivores

How big was it?
It was the length of two cars and weighed a little more than two grizzly bears.

What did it eat?
It was an herbivore and had sharp teeth for ripping up plants.

Funny fact:
Plateosaurus's brain was pretty small compared to its body, so it probably wasn't the brightest!

Where was it found?
Nuremberg, Germany, by the fossil hunter Hermann von Meyer

ONE OF THE FIRST DINOS ON THE SCENE!

EORAPTOR
(meaning "dawn thief")

How do I say that?
EE-oh-RAP-tor

How big was it?
A bit taller than a chicken, and twice the weight of a cat

Did you know?
Its jaw contained a mix of teeth: long and sharp up front, leaf-shaped in the back.

What did it eat?
It was an omnivore, eating meat and plants. It even chowed down on insects and stolen eggs.

When did it live?
228,000,000 years ago. It's one of the earliest dinos that sped around Pangaea!

Where was it found?
Valle de la Luna (Valley of the Moon), Argentina

COELOPHYSIS

(meaning "hollow form" as it had hollow bones!)

How do I say that?
Coh-ell-oh-FIE-sis

Unusually large eyes

How big was it?
9 feet (3 m) long, 3 feet (1 m) high. It weighed the same as you!

What did it eat?
It was a carnivore.

Where was it found?
Ghost Ranch Quarry, New Mexico

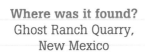

Funny fact:
So many Coelophysis samples have been found in New Mexico that they have made it their state fossil!

EUSKELOSAURUS

(meaning "good leg dinosaur")

How do I say that?
YOO-skel-oh-SORE-us

How big was it?
It was one of the largest Triassic dinosaurs. It was almost as long
as a bus and weighed a little less than a rhinoceros!

What do you call a
dino in high heels?

What did it eat?
It was an herbivore. It was a semi-bipedal
creature, meaning it walked on all four
limbs, but could support itself on two legs
when reaching up for leaves on high trees.

My-feet-are-saurus!

**Twisted
femur
bone**

Funny fact:
Strangely, its thigh bone (called
the femur) was twisted, leading
experts to believe that the back
legs of the Euskelosaurus
were "bow-legged."

Where was it found?
South Africa, Lesotho, and Botswana.

STAURIKOSAURUS

(meaning "southern cross reptile")

How do I say that?
STOR-ik-oh-SORE-us

How big was it?
Human-sized, and twice the weight of a bowling ball

What did it eat?
It fed on small animals.

Did you know?
It's called a bipedal dinosaur. That means it could support itself on two legs.

Lived 200,000,000 years ago!

Where was it found?
Brazil, South America

What did it eat?
It was a meat-eater!

Did you know?
The Liliensternus was a great hunter, with five long fingers; sharp, curved claws; pointed teeth; and a powerful jaw.

Where was it found?
In wetlands and forest, in what is now Germany.

Fin-like crest

LILIENSTERNUS

This dinosaur was named after the German scientist Dr Hugo Rule von Lilienstern.

How do I say that?
LIL-ee-en-STERN-us

How big was it?
One of the largest predators of the Triassic period, it was three times longer than your bed!

JUMPING TO THE JURASSIC!

We're waving goodbye to the Triassic period and taking a look at what happened next. Let's step back 200 million years and begin the next chapter of our dinosaur adventure!

What were the hot topics in the 64 million year-long Jurassic period? Remember the map in Home Sweet Home? The giant continent it depicted, Pangaea, split up into Laurasia and, eventually, Gondwana. These continents continued to drift until they formed the ones we know today.

It's got me feeling dizzy!

What happened to the massive ocean, Panthalassa?
The ocean moved too as these continents drifted. Huge lagoons and lakes flooded the spaces that were left when the land moved apart.

What kind of world did the dinos rule?
Earth was changing. The rising sea levels meant that the hot and dry planet was becoming humid and damp. Dry deserts turned green, and conifer trees, ginkgoes, and cycads flourished. Lush vegetation meant that the booming dinosaur population never went hungry!

What other creatures were hanging out in the Jurassic period?
Look up! There's the *Archaeopteryx* (**AR-kee-OP-ter-icks**), Earth's "first bird."

This story might have wings. (Ha ha!) What was Archaeopteryx like?
The pigeon-sized Archaeopteryx is what's called a "transitional" animal. Although this creature had feathers and wings, it held onto some trademark dino features such as teeth, claws, and a long bony tail. Let's fly over to the next page and discover more Jurassic residents.

APATOSAURUS
(meaning "deceptive lizard")

It munched 800 pounds (360 kilos) of food a day!

How do I say that?
ah-PAT-oh-SORE-us

How old did it get?
This old-timer probably reached its hundredth birthday.

What did it eat?
It was an herbivore, swallowing plants whole.

A long tail to help it balance

Did you know?
The Apatosaurus laid huge eggs. At one foot (.3 m) tall, these egg-cellent specimens were the size of a basketball!

Where was it found?
Colorado, Oklahoma, Utah, and Wyoming, USA

STEGOSAURUS
(meaning "roof lizard")

bony plates

4 spikes on its tail

How do I say that?
STEG-oh-SORE-us

How big was it?
As long as three polar bears, and as heavy as a car

What did it eat?
It wolfed down plants near the ground, as it had a short neck.

Where was it found?
Western USA. It's the state dinosaur of Colorado.

Brain Power:
Probably not bright! Its brain was the size of a walnut.

Distinctive features:
A double row of bony plates along its back, and four spikes on its tail. Fossil hunters think that the plates were for showing off or controlling temperatures. The spikes were used to whack attackers!

MEGALOSAURUS

(meaning "great lizard")
It was the first dinosaur to be named!

How do I say that?
MEG-ah-low-SORE-us

How big was it?
Twice as heavy as a grand piano, and nearly four times as long.

What did it eat?
Meat. It was a first-class hunter.

Where was it found?
Oxfordshire, England

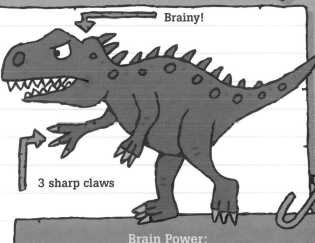

Brainy!

3 sharp claws

Brain Power:
Super-smart! Not only was its brain-to-body ratio high, but also, scientists believed it both hunted down small prey and scavenged dead animals—whatever it could find!

Did you know?
Part of a Megalosaurus bone was first found over 300 years ago, in an English quarry. At first, old-time experts thought it was the thigh bone from a giant human.

DIPLODOCUS

This means "double beam," named after the two rows of bones supporting its super-long tail!

How do I say that?
DIP-low-DOCK-us

Flat, blunt teeth

What did it eat?
This herbivore had peg-like teeth, for stripping leaves and ferns.

How big was it?
Huge! It was longer than a tennis court, and heavier than three and a half hippos.

Did you know?
It's thought that the Diplodocus held its neck in a horizontal position, just 17 feet (5 meters) off the ground. If the dino had held its head vertically, experts believe that pumping blood up its 21-foot (6.5 m) neck, thousands of times a day, would have been too much for the poor Diplodocus' heart.

Long tail for balance, with over 80 vertebrae

Small head and long neck

Where was it found?
Colorado, Montana, Utah, and Wyoming, USA

BRACHIOSAURUS

(meaning "arm lizard")

How do I say that?
BRAYK-ee-oh-SORE-us

How big was it?
Taller than a four-story house, but a tenth of the weight of a blue whale

What did it eat?
The Brachiosaurus had very long front legs, allowing it to feed from high trees. That was lucky, as this herbivore needed to snack on 440 pounds of vegetation every single day!

Where was it found?
Western USA

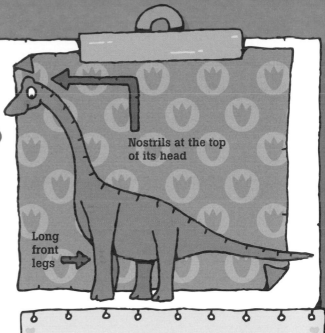

Nostrils at the top of its head

Long front legs

Fascinating Fact:
Like many sauropods, Brachiosaurus's fossilized bones are often found without its head. This is a real pain in the neck when trying to identify dino remains!

ALLOSAURUS

(This means "different lizard." At the time of its discovery, the Allosaurus's backbone wasn't like that of any other dino.)

How do I say that?
AL-oh-SORE-us

How long did it live?
About 28 years. It reached full adult size by the age of 15 years.

Where was it found?
Utah, Colorado, and Texas, USA

It weighed up to 4.5 tons!

Super-sharp teeth

What did it eat?
This carnivore was the biggest meat-eater in North America during the whole of the Jurassic period.

Did you know?
There's proof that the Allosaurus and Stegosaurus weren't the best of buddies. Exhibit A is an Allosaurus back bone with a Stegosaurus spike-shaped hole. Exhibit B is a Stegosaurus neck bone with an Allosaurus-shaped bite mark!

WHO RAN THE WORLD? DINOS!

Whiz back 145 million years, and see what the Cretaceous period has to offer.

How did Earth develop over the next 80 million years?
By the end of the Cretaceous period, 65 million years ago, the world was looking a lot more familiar. South America and Africa had taken shape, although India had not yet bumped into Asia and Australia was still stuck to Antarctica.

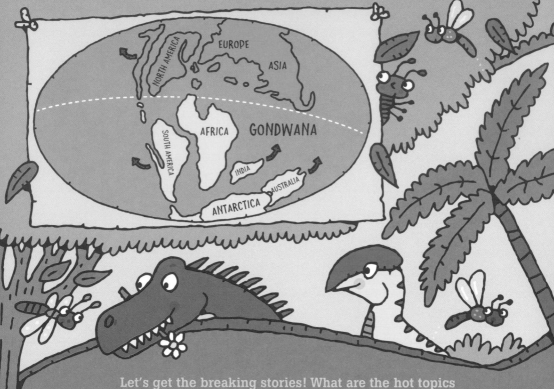

Let's get the breaking stories! What are the hot topics from the Cretaceous Communications Desk?

Is there any good news for prehistoric plant-eaters?
The first flowering plants arrived! Trees began to produce flowers, and magnolia and maple trees sprung up. What a treat for the hungry herbivores!

What was the buzz in the animal kingdom?
The Cretaceous period was crawling with moths, bees, termites, and ants. They helped to spread the pollen from flower to flower, multiplying these blooming specimens until they soon outnumbered the ferns, conifers, ginkgoes, and cycads.

What are the bulletins from the beach?

Sea levels were higher during this period than at any other time in Earth's history. Giant marine reptiles filled the seas, which covered 82% of the world's surface, compared with 72% today. Much of the Midwest USA was underwater, as evidenced today by the many fossils of sea creatures in this region.

How was the Cretaceous climate?

This period saw the warmest conditions Earth had ever experienced. The toasty sea temperatures reached a mild 95 degrees Fahrenheit (35 degrees Celsius), and the North and South Poles were ice-free! Phew!

The Cretaceous period was a booming time for the dinosaurs! Let's take a snapshot of these weird and wonderful creatures!

GIGANOTOSAURUS

(meaning "giant southern lizard," not gigantic lizard as some people think!)

How do I say that?
JIG-ah-NO-toe-SORE-us

How fast did it run?
Experts calculate that the Giganotosaurus would have clocked up speeds of 25-30 mph. That's about the same as a fit rider on a good bike!

What did it eat?
Meat...which it sliced and diced with long, serrated teeth!

Brain power:
Its brain was the size and shape of a small banana, even though its head was bigger than a fridge. I'll let you draw your own conclusions.

Where was it found?
Argentina, South America

(It's thought that the Giganotosaurus may have hunted the awesome Argentinosaurus in packs.)

VELOCIRAPTOR
(meaning "swift thief")

Retractable claws →

How do I say that?
ve-LAW-suh-RAP-tor

What did it eat?
It was carnivorous, and maybe a scavenger too!

How big was it?
The length of a bed, and three times as heavy as a cat

What was its secret weapon?
It had curved, razor-sharp claws on its hind feet, which it would use to slash, jab, and rip apart its prey.

Did you know?
A famous fossil discovery featured Velociraptor mid-fight with a Protoceratops. Who do you think would've won?

Where was it found? Mongolia, Asia

ARGENTINOSAURUS

How do I say that?
AR-gen-TEEN-oh-SORE-us

How big was it?
Enormous! It was longer than a blue whale, and taller than a two-story building. Its weight was a third of the Statue of Liberty!

What did it eat?
Plants! In fact, this herbivore is currently in first place as the largest plant-eating dino.

Fascinating fact:
After hatching from a beach ball-sized egg, it would take decades for these mini dinos to reach their adult dimensions. The baby Argentinosaurus had to grow 25,000 times its original size!

Where was it found?
The clue's in the name!

Take a look at these Cretaceous creatures! Do you think you can memorize these fascinating facts and figures?

TYRANNOSAURUS REX
(meaning "tyrant lizard king")

How do I say that?
tie-RAN-ah-SORE-us REX

How big was it?
It was as tall as a giraffe,
but over 4.5 times heavier.

What did it eat?
It could eat over 500 pounds of meat
in one chomp and could even crunch
through bone. Fragments of its victims'
bones have been found in fossilized
Tyrannosaurus poop!

Don't mention:
Its feeble arms. We don't know why these
arms were so puny. Here are some suggestions:

1. Neck and arm muscles were in competition for space,
and the neck muscles won!

2. Long arms are vulnerable in an attack, and could easily be
broken. Short arms use less energy.

3. They only needed their arms to lever themselves off the ground
after a nap or a knock-out blow.

4. Actually, you're being very rude. Although their stumpy
arms look ridiculous, they're actually the size of an average
four-year-old and packed with muscle.

Where was it found?
Montana, Texas, Wyoming, Utah, USA

TRICERATOPS

Bony frill to guard its neck

Here's a test! Think back! Do you remember what this dinosaur's name means?

How do I say that?
tri-SAIR-ah-tops

How big was it?
30 feet long (9 m). The length of its skull was a third of its entire body.

What did it eat?
The triceratops would chew and nibble through tough leaves with its horned beak and shearing teeth.

Fascinating facts:
Triceratops's horns were likely covered in a protein called *keratin.* You have it in your fingernails too!

Where was it found?
Colorado, and other western USA and Canadian sites

SPINOSAURUS

(No prizes for guessing! Its name means "spine lizard.")

How do I say that?
SPINE-uh-SORE-us

Longer arms than most two-legged meat eaters

How big was it?
As long as five bottle-nosed dolphins. It may have been the largest carnivorous dino ever!

What did it eat?
Small mammals, fish, and other delicious dinosaurs

Distinctive features:
Its spines were the height of a basketball player. They could have been used to control body temperature, or to support a camel-like hump containing supplies of fat or fluid. Or it might have helped the Spinosaurus navigate through water, or simply to show off.

Where was it found?
Egypt and Morocco

SO LONG! FAREWELL!

The Cretaceous period ends with a bang: There's an emergency on Earth, which spells disaster for the dinosaurs.

What made the dinos disappear?
Scientists have calculated that dinos died out around 65 million years ago. They've also discovered that, at the same time, an asteroid from space crashed into Earth in Mexico.

What did this asteroid do to the planet?
Let's look at the experts' facts and figures. The asteroid was six miles wide, hit Earth at 40,000 miles per hour, and released more energy than any nuclear bomb ever made. The horrendous heat would have ignited forest fires, and clouds of debris would have plunged the planet into darkness. Earthquakes and volcanoes would be activated and huge tidal waves, called *tsunamis*, would have swept animals away.

What did this mean for the dinos?
No light means no plants! Herbivores would have starved, and the carnivores would soon have no herbivores to feast on.

Which dinos made the best police officers?

tricera-cops!

Science hot-shots are looking into alternative explanations for the (deep breath) *Cretaceous-Tertiary mass extinction*, or *K/T extinction* for short. It could have been a mass eruption of volcanoes in India, blasting out molten rock and gas and making the oceans acidic. Other ideas under discussion include a plague that spread through the dino population, an ice age that the dinos couldn't cope with, or irritating mammals continually stealing dinosaur eggs, slowly making them extinct.

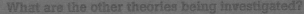

FACT OR FICTION

Were ALL animal species wiped out in the mass extinction?
No! Welcome to the K/T Extinction Survivors Club, and say hi to crocodiles, alligators, birds, frogs, lizards, snakes, turtles, and mammals!

How did they survive?
First, they could escape the extreme, temporary heat by burrowing underground or diving beneath the waves. Second, their diet didn't depend on massive amounts of plants. Third, they could snack on insects or sea plants, some of which flourished after the planet's meltdown.

WELCOME

I SURVIVED THE K/T EXTINCTION

SURVIVOR

I SURVIVED THE K/T EXTINCTION

DOWN AT THE DINO DIG!

Grab your hammer, chisel, and safety glasses and join us as we hunt for fossils! Let's see what buried secrets we can uncover!

> Let's speed things up!

First things first! What is a fossil?

It is the preserved remains of an animal or plant. Most dinosaur fossils take shape when the creature's remains turn into stone. For example, a dino may die and be buried by mud. The tissues of its body are replaced by minerals, dissolved in water. These minerals turn into stone, and the surrounding mud turns into rock. This process can take millions of years.

> Why do museums display old dinosaur bones?

> they can't afford new ones

What is a trace fossil?

A trace fossil is the evidence of a dinosaur's activity, such as a footprint, eggs, or even poop! They show us a lot about dino behavior.

What can a dinosaur fossil teach us?

We get oodles of data from fossil hunting, or *paleontology*. Experts can calculate a dino's height, width, and weight. Scientists can figure out what a dino ate from its teeth and estimate how fast it ran and how it may have hunted from its leg structure. They can even guess at a dino's IQ by measuring its brain-to-body ratio.

Where are the best locations for dinosaur hunting?

Take a look at the map! Dino remains have been discovered all around the world.
Some are buried underground, but others are exposed by wind, rain, or landslides.

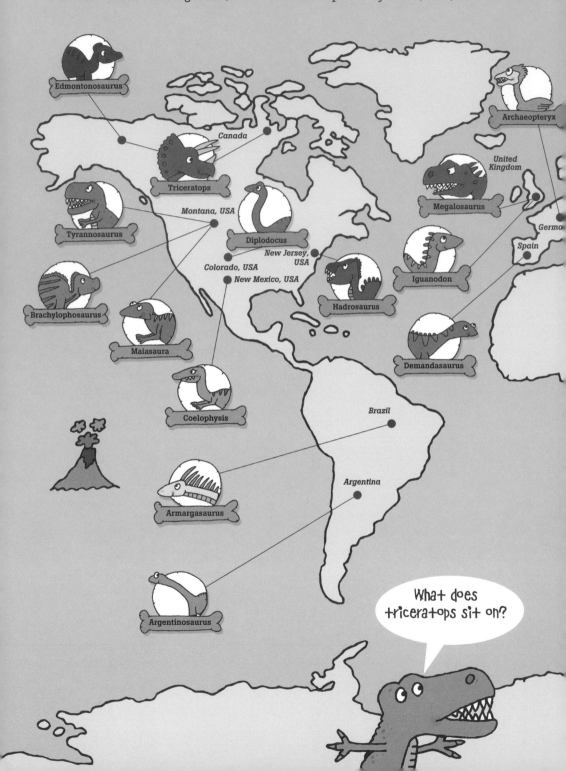

Velociraptor

Sinosauropteryx

Russia

China

Spinosaurus

Confuciusornis

Egypt

Thailand

Isanosaurus

Tanzania

Giraffatitan

Australia

Muttaburrasaurus

South
Africa

Heterodontosaurus

Cryolophosaurus

Its tricera-
bottom!

Antarctica

47

IT'S ALL RELATIVE!

Do we share the planet with dinosaur descendants? Could there be a happy ending after all?

Is there a link between living creatures and dinos that have bitten the dust?

It's true! Current research suggests that birds probably evolved from two-legged theropods, such as *Velociraptor*. In recent years, fossil hunters have discovered an astonishing surprise: a number of dinosaurs with quills and hairy bristles. It's now suspected that feathers evolved in dinosaurs, way before birds hopped along!

THE WING TO-DO LIST

What other changes took place?
The theropods' arms and digits evolved to form a wing joint, their bones became lighter, tails formed a stump and established tail feathers, and the creatures became toothless.

How did ancient birds avoid getting their tail feathers burnt during the dinosaur extinction?
They were smaller and more adaptable to their changing environment, allowing them to outlast their larger relatives. With the bigger dinos out of the way, smaller ones could rule the roost!

When should you buy a bird?

When it's going cheep!

CHECK OUT ALL OF THE FANTASTIC FACTS IN THIS SENSATIONAL SERIES!